Encouraged by a positive respons[...]
Mermaid is Unimpressed", I have d[...]
events, fancies and strange coinci[...]
volume. Since last May I have been the recipient of mysterious letters from the Merzey Island Chapter of Merpersons (tucked under my cousin's windscreen wipers in Colchester — what cheek!), some wonderful verses from appreciative readers sharing the joy and a few sideways glances. I will continue to ignore the latter.

My thanks again to my husband Sean, my most critical reader, to Philip Bell at Beachy Books for his encouragement and hard work and to Shaun Cuff for digging the lady out again and sending her down the Military Road on a Harley.

Enjoy.

Sandy Realty

First published by Beachy Books in 2020
www.beachybooks.com

A catalogue record for this book is available from the British Library.

ISBN: 978-1-9997283-4-2

Set in Palatino

The Mermaid Rides Again

Sandy Kealty

BEACHY BOOKS

Contents

I concluded my first book "The Mermaid is Unimpressed" with a promise of motor bikes, caution and hip hop. Here is how the relationship with bikes began. You may also recognise a warning note.

Riding Pillion

When I was young, my father bought a Francis Barnett;
sober, made in England,
fairing, for protection and performance,
giving it a piggish look.
There began acceptance of a life
of hopping on behind.

Some rides were punishing.
Two hundred miles at dead of night,
(the traffic's lighter then),
arriving sore and frozen at my grandma's;
my turn, that year, to save the fare.

Some rides made sense.
We'd blow away the cobwebs at weekends,
deferring homework and the sanctuary of the shed,
find time to eat ice cream and talk a little,
to modify our growing discontent with one another.

I ask myself, what might have been the outcome
had I become a rider, mistress of my own machine?
Would I have spent less time a follower,
no clinging on, no perching pillion,
my chicken strips a source of wonder,
my attitude more independently inclined?

The epic summer journey was to Tankerton in Kent. Whitstable boasted oysters and Peter Cushing, but Tankerton had The Street, a half-mile spit of shingle running straight out to sea at low tide. Irresistible.

Tankerton Street

My grandfather found some remnants of Rome,
took them home.
Bits of clay pipes, discarded from barges,
buttons and bones.
Shells, combs, oddly-shaped stones,
on Tankerton Street.

Our treat, during days at the beach hut,
was to scavenge its length as the water went down.
If you fail to go right to the end you're a pussy,
don't care if you think you might drown
when the tide ambles back,
over star fish and bladderwrack,
cockles and winkles and wonderful worms,
to reclaim them for old Davy Jones.

The Street is so bare now, no items of interest,
and flattish and muddy to boot.
Perhaps Swale and Thames meet at angles quite different,
perhaps sea defences have altered the tide,
perhaps there is nothing to loot.

Should we leave mermaids' tears
where the mermaids once wept?
Should we leave them alone?

When I moved to the Isle of Wight as a mature bride, my interest in motorbikes was rekindled. My new husband is a skilled and careful rider, but we did have an unfortunate incident.

On Taking a Sudden Tumble from a Bike

Kawasaki GPZ eleven hundred,
down the Mili' Road with a noise like thunder.
"Is this suitable for me?" I sort of wondered,
thought I'd be ok, but my days were numbered.
I don't bounce anymore.

Big and black and Japanese, so comfortable and broad,
when we felt like trips to teashops, we'd climb on board,
go in search of calories we couldn't quite afford,
for when you've been at work all week, you need a reward.
I don't bounce anymore.

Perched up on the back, I'm no civilian,
I've done the ton down Dover Straight without my coat on.
If I've taken one risk recently, I've taken a million,
but there's not much to hold on to when you're riding pillion.
I don't bounce any more.

They told me in the hospital that I'd been lucky,
though I'm cut about a bit, it's not gone mucky,
and I'll learn to walk quite normally, if I'm plucky.
"You'll know better than to ride again, won't you, ducky!
You don't bounce any more."

Perhaps I should be wise,
but there is a compromise;
halvies with a girlfriend on a custom trike,
with a dog and a bandana,
I'll keep carrying the banner,
might not bounce, but I can flounce …

I'll think about it later, when my leg's not sore.

Recovery gave me the leisure to reflect on past stratagems for survival.

The Scent of Times Gone By

Lamb was the worst, meaty miasma,
haunting the wallpaper until Monday,
serving as remembrance that we'd not
joined in tribal babble at the family table,
as others did.

Nobody had had the gall to chirrup,
"God bless us, every one!"
Silence was mandatory
and the vegetables cold,
like vengeance.

Our father spent his weekends in the shed,
with lathe and band-saw, jars of tidy screws,
which qualified him, in his manliness,
to portion out the Sunday meat
and sharpen knives.

Snick! Snack!

"Oh do come in and carve, my love!
We've waited half an hour.
That's surely long enough, my love
to demonstrate your power."

I found myself the perfect job,
moral high ground, unassailable work ethic,
cooked Sunday lunch for forty chattering lads
at one of Malvern's many prep schools.
They washed up, while I prepared their tea,
pulled leeks and lettuce from the kitchen garden,
cleaned the eggs.

I learned some higher skills:
to decorate a fish baked whole,
to gently pipe out Melting Moments,
to ignore the pheasants rotting in the larder.
This was not my world,
but how it served as sanctuary.

I carried home my own scent,
exhausted sweat,
held my nose up high.

I even had a moment to ponder the nature of time itself,
how slippery it is, how fleeting.

If I Could Weave a Net

If I could weave a net to capture time,
I would, provided that the weather's fine,
snare some unwanted early hours, when day is breaking,
and wrap them in a morning smell of baking.
I'd store them in my secret cave
for later distribution to the sad, the brave, the dispossessed,
and we would have a festival once in a while;
though I would also like to save some time
that would be very clearly labelled "mine".

If I could weave a net to capture time,
I'd snatch the hours that we simply waste
in dull-eyed serfdom to the current taste
for life dumbed down, homogenised,
bereft of quality, but supersized,
and, using my new time machine,
I'd process them beyond your wildest dreams.
I'd stretch them, polish them and make them gleam,
then everyone would have a share. I'd not be mean.
And when I ask, "How was your day?",
the answer would outshine the usual "Fine.",
for you would smile a radiant smile and say, "Sublime!"

If I could weave that net,
you'd never have to ask where years have gone,
for, with my harvested additions,
there would be time to spare.
It is my strong submission that you might
put better moments in your pocket
for re-examination later. No, don't mock!
It's practical to thus recycle time that we have valued,
to unwind it, savour it and roll it up again.

"How time does fly!" will be my call to arms,
for it will set off loud alarms at my headquarters.
I will cast the net
and, in a trice, I'd stop time in its tracks,
then firmly, gently, give it back.

How I'd be honoured, loved and feted,
respected by all those to whom I'd demonstrated
my great invention.
I do believe the Queen would ask me round to dine
if I could weave a net to capture time.

Of course I remounted, but my dear friend Moira thought I needed more protection, and my man bought a bike more suited to my age and stature. The final three stanzas must be sung, I'm afraid. If permitted, a Hispanic accent would not go amiss. Thank you Mr Bernstein.

Return of the Bling

I never had such a jacket.
So thick, so slick,
so strapped and zipped
and wrapped and nipped
at the waist and broad in the shoulder,
so heavy; if I were a little bit older
and frailer and a total wet hen,
why then,
I couldn't wear it at all.

Dear Moira, who knows me better than most,
thought maybe I'd stand the ghost
of a chance clad in good thick leather,
against inclement weather
and impact with the highway.
She'd never need to wear it again,
so she passed it my way.
She's a great mate,
it's what she would say,
for she knows that a brush with death
is a mere bagatelle to a Warrior Princess;
Go to hell all those who say I'll rue it,
with your cries of "Don't do it! Don't do it! Don't do it!"
The Leader of the Pack
is back.

You see …
We've bought a Triumph America,
it's sweet and it's neat, it's angelic a
cruiser, no loser, so swell, it's a
pulling machine, Sí, es muy bella!

He traded his racer for this one,
he wanted us both to still have fun,
I needed a mount that was low slung,
well this fits the bill, it was well done!

We ride a Triumph America,
a Trumpet, a strumpet, a hell raiser.
At home, see the chrome, he will polish her,
a magnet for babes, es magnifica!

Alas, there have been other setbacks involving surgery but there are always compensatory factors. You are allowed to run for the hills at the end of this poem.

Convalescence 2013

Eight weeks at least, they told me,
maybe more.
With clinics and a public holiday,
the score went up to ten;
a munificence of time,
"That's fine," I said, and made a list.

There's writing, needing just that bit more work,
those scribbles, crying out for immortality,
boxes mouldering beneath the stairs
since I put them there ten years ago;
the dressing up clothes, my grandfather's diaries,
the music box that should be sold,
abandoned, pressing for my notice.

But I bought a ukulele, nearly learned to play it,
designed a brand new garden, grew some beans,
read playful books and loafed about,
and idled days away,
a shame they were much shorter than they seemed.

I ignored the recommended works I'd not had time to read,
tomes pickled in gravitas,
though some have been downloaded to the Kindle,
another list in waiting.

I ignored the eight track techie stuff I bought last year.
The CD is not imminent.
Didn't sort my photos,
make up playlists,
pay visits long overdue.

No, I bought a ukulele, nearly learned to play it,
walked down to the duck pond,
stood and stared.
I watched the sunlight on the wall,
and did a lot of bugger all.
I'm duty bound to tell you,
you deserve to be prepared,
I bought a ukulele, now I'll play it.

I may also have done some gentle needlework. It's something I enjoy and I was fortunate to be set on that path early in life. I found the tray cloth sixty-five years later amongst my mother's things.

Going Bad

Stitches not quite up to snuff;
straight as a desert road
but lacking uniformity.
There was an undoing, my third, I fear,
with concomitant tutting.

Miss B, from Birmingham,
confined and disenchanted,
steward of Girls' Needlework, year three,
appeared to be in need of consolation.
Obliging, I consulted her
on suitable embellishment of the tray cloth,
once current difficulties were overcome.

"Ducks," I offered, smiling, "blue on green water,
or maybe green on blue."
The dust motes stilled.

"Blue and green should never be seen," she hissed,
a mantra quite unknown to me.
I thought of bluebells and delphiniums
and, two weeks later, crafted ducks
in jewelled colours, as discussed.

The finished cloth was placed with love
in Mother's treasure drawer.
Miss B abandoned teaching, preaching,
reaching for harmonious perfection,
married, moved away.

I'm looking for a tray.

I caught up with some old films and drew some conclusions.

Vested Interest

There is nothing like Bruce Willis in a vest.
There is something rare about him that outshines all the rest.
Say I've got my silly head on,
but when I see Armageddon,
or Die Hard 1 to 3,
something strange comes over me.
I'm utterly, outrageously impressed.

There's a lesser sort of fever
when I see Sigourney Weaver
fighting acid-dripping aliens in space.
Lighter clothing is a must,
it's really all I'd trust
in the confines of a nasty, sticky, claustrophobic place.

Yes, I'll stick to my contention,
and I'll brook no cruel dissension.
When declaring one's intention,
vest is best.

I fell to wondering what I can offer when it comes to Saving
the World.

Snippet

I cannot let a pretty piece of velvet go.
I find it difficult to throw
the things for which I'm now too fat.
I rescue gems from other people's tat.
I mend and alter, sew on buttons.
I am an unrepentant glutton
for changing hemlines.
I'd like to darn, but that's too sad,
but once I could, and would be pleased
to find my mushroom once again,
to renovate the socks that might remain
when climate change leaves us bereft of shops.
Yes, then I'd gladly pull out all the stops.

Time to reflect upon a battle lost.

In Memoriam

I found it lying in a gutter,
utter perfection in its size and shape,
substantial, shiny, full of promise.
Oh, what a fighter it would make!
No mightier in all my playground world.

Shame I could only dash the pride of fellow female cognoscenti!
The boys at Somers Park were cordoned off
behind a high brick wall.
But I knew there would be challenges a-plenty,
and I would beat them all.

With utmost care, measuring by half-closed eye,
I screwed the skewer through its centre,
drinking in the wild and woody raw-nut smell,
cushioning the oily shell,
no damage done;
and so for string.

It must be new, no saved, recycled scrappy stuff would do.
The knots were elegant, the balance true.

It was a thing of beauty and a joy 'til breakfast.

My brother saw it by the cornflakes.
My brother smiled a smile.
He made a sound, the sound that scorn makes,
and left me for a while.

Returned with wizened, seasoned, vinegar-embalmed,
renowned campaigner in his hand.
I made my stand.

A whacking thwack that jarred my wrist,
a sickening crack, and so I kissed
goodbye to my pretensions.

A drizzly walk to school, alone, forlorn,
a fitting sort of day to mourn
my poor divided conker.

And battles yet to come. This with many thanks to the late Jeremy Hardy, who, on the News Quiz in May 2019, announced his intention to dress as a Valkyrie to attend the end of the world.

Ragnarök

I am going to the end of the world as a Valkyrie.
There won't be time to grow my hair,
so, along with tins of soup, air freshener and ammunition,
I will make sure I have a large blonde wig.
(Some folk, I see, are wearing theirs already.
Should I expedite my order?)
I have sourced a hornèd helmet on the internet;
with Prime I could be kitted out tomorrow.

I feel I should give passing thought
to anxious guardians of correct behaviour.
Without a doubt, the family, on both sides,
by way of Taunton, Kent and Chichester,
descend from goodly Viking stock.
I had an Uncle Eric.
My grandmother had auburn locks.

But if you do suspect an error,
lay bare my cultural appropriation,
and Twitter out the last of days.

I mount my ethereal steed,
secure my feathered cloak,
choose who I'll save.
We'll soon be gone.

When I decided it was time to come to life again after my widowing, I turned to an agency to find suitable companionship. We didn't have the internet back then. I had an interview with a sympathetic lady and parted with £300. Unfortunately, she wasn't listening.

Hand Matched 1

Over lunch, I gathered we'd not much in common,
apart from loneliness.
He was a milkman, who spent daytime hours
restoring windmills.

I thought of the mornings;
don't wake until seven.
Don't think I'd manage
a sweet smile at four.

I thought of the windmills
and slow reconstruction.
I thought of the dust,
of the spiders, and more.
I thought of the gatherings
of earnest enthusiasts.
I thought of it all.

I showed him the door.

The next adventure was more productive, but I continued
to wonder which of my characteristics had been considered
back at the agency.

Hand Matched 2

A gentle soul, who kept a buzzard
tethered to a hoop out in the yard.
The implications here did not escape me,
but this was just his opening card.
He'd made a cake to sweeten our first conversation,
chocolate, which I detest, with just a tiny taste of lard.

He'd been a serial husband, four times in all,
and knew what attributes should come with number five.
We decided, with astounding swiftness,
I was too posh, too arrogant, too opinionated
to be added to his list of wives.

I still had all my feathers, functioning wings.
He needed someone to admire him,
cook, agree and warm his bed.

But he was friendly.
We swapped lawn mowers.
Mine was much too big for me and he said his was very small.
He took my pond, which I was not prepared to care for.
It wasn't total failure, after all.

He persevered.
He met his bride on holiday in Thailand,
and then his friend from round the corner
brought her younger sibling home!

The ladies visited each other daily,
to confer, to plot, to play.
What a dance those sisters led them,
but the boys just let them have their way.
Fed and bedded, buzzard watered;
lucky number five, I say.

I hesitated over the next tale, but it does serve to illustrate
the diversity of the choices available.

Hand Matched 3

It went so well.
A meal, a walk, a visit to the theatre,
but then I found out, for less public leisure,
his pleasure was to be bound fast, tight as tight.
How serendipitous that, in the past,
I had spent evenings with a Scouting man,
who taught me clove hitch, bowline, double carrick bend.

For extra treats, he did propose a gag.
I balanced this against a lively mind,
and yes, to tell the truth, the Jag,
decided it would be unkind
to cast a cloud on his parade.

But I'm afraid there came a time
when ennui overcame me.
I wandered off to make a cup of tea,
and clean forgot where I had left him,
immobilised in such a cunning web of string,
(Akela would have thought it just the thing),
fashioned lovingly, in fun,
but not so easily undone.

However hard I tried to make amends,
the tie unravelled and we met less often.
Now, I doubt we even count as friends.

But hope springs eternal, and, as I remarked to my spouse just the other day, the gorse is in bloom.

A Page From My Almanac

The gorse is in bloom.
Though my room's full of shadows at four,
and the sky is as grey as the stare of a parson,
and my fingers are raw with remains of a chilblain,
the gorse is in bloom.

Up by the bay,
you can smell the rough water,
the wind comes from somewhere near Novosibirsk,
gathering malice and fretful discomfort,
but the gorse is in bloom.

It may not be rational but fashion dictates
that when gorse is in bloom it's the right time to mate,
or at least to trade kisses to store up for later.
Look, the gorse is in bloom!

Don't be fooled by the obvious stuffy riposte
that somewhere it blooms all year round, you'll be lost;
for the right time to heed the old wives' advice
is all year, at all times; though it's specially nice
when the joy of that bustling, bright golden flower
contrasts with the sadness of midwinter glower.
Dear, the gorse is in bloom.

But we must beware of making assumptions. Sometimes trouble springs up unexpectedly. I wrote this one to appease a colleague who had objected to my use of a common Latin tag. He was studying law at the time.

Mea Culpa

Mea culpa, I've upset you,
wasn't really out to get you.
De profundis, I'm so sorry,
I'll throw myself beneath a lorry.
Dulce et decorum est
to be the same as all the rest.
Tempus fugit … so must I,
the Grammar Schools deserved to die.
Erase those thoughts of grace and beauty,
make all things grey … it is your duty,
et tu Brute.

My ability to get things wrong was developed in early childhood.

Unoriginal Sin

Her people smacked of laissez faire;
bohemians or something in the theatre.
They were certainly above their station,
rarely cleaned their windows, never mowed.

She was a bold-faced drama queen,
told me she had a wooden foot.
There was no evidence, no bolts or hinges
showing through her greyish socks,
but I felt sorry for her just the same,
as we nested in the long grass of her back garden
and snacked on stolen Farley's rusks.

She was a weaver of yarns,
delicious in the after-school sun.
I was fascinated, sought her company,
although I had been told to shun her.

There had to be a reckoning.

I avoided the blow,
but my mother fished me out, delivered it,
accused me of illicit meetings
with people of the lower sort.

Guilty as charged but puzzled,
for no one in my short existence had advised
that "Sod it!" was, in some way, wrong.
I was struck, not for the last time,
by the unreasonableness of life.

I skulked to my grandmother's bedroom,
refused tea, refused conversation.
None of it mattered anyway,
for I had eaten the burning red end
of a sweet cigarette that day,
and I was going to die.
Sue told me.

I believe I promised to refer to caution in this second book.
The next poem deals with a dangerous person. Be nice to her.

Winning Ways

"Prithee give me your seat, O young, pretty maid!"
sang the crone on the fifty nine bus.
The maid fixed the crone with a cold, fierce stare,
then blew down her nose and flicked back her hair,
and responded disdainfully thus:

"You are old and revolting, with everything sagging,
it must be the weight of your fat.
Your bones are too feeble to back up your nagging;
bet you live all alone with a cat !
It's a long way to town and I want to sit down.
I've paid for my seat, so I'll sit in it.
You have a free pass … and quite frankly, your arse
is so big that I doubt that you'd fit in it."

Her protagonist uttered a quavering, "But!"

"Shut your face, you old bat!"
said the maid who had paid.

Then round the old lady, a strange mist arose,
she wiggled her fingers and scrunched up her nose,
she pulled the chin whisker that looked so absurd,
and she muttered a troublesome word.

In a flash,
on the seat,
that the maid
bought with cash,
was a large
tin of meat
labelled CAT,
I'm afraid.

The old lady sat with a smile and a sigh,
tucked the tin in her trundling bag.
"I'll feed her to Tabby tonight, as a treat.
My Tabs doesn't think I'm a hag.
Despicable child of despicable Thatcher,
Watch out that the witch on the bus doesn't catch yer!"

Did I ever tell you about the time I moved North and became a Working Man? If not, you may need a little note about meat raffles. "Winning the box" is high English irony. The box is empty, for the meat it contained has all been distributed to holders of more propitious tickets.

Becoming a Working Man

The stairs are narrow, dark and steep.
We hug the wall as up we creep.
From those ascending, worried frowns,
a smile from those folk coming down.

I clasp my partner's hand.
Will our accents betray us?
We are from the South.
Will there be questions about the meat raffle?
I won the box when we stopped off in Burnley.
I found it hard to understand the applause.

The stairs are narrow, steep and dark.
We only did it for a lark,
thought it would help our integration.
Now we face interrogation.

We enter the room.
Three gruff men consider our loyalty,
our sobriety and the likelihood of her on the distaff side
inhabiting the wrong bar at the wrong time,
where men are men and talk is rough.

Things may have changed by now,
but sequestration in a separate place
had irked me as we travelled north
and had a need to slake our thirst.

I hold my tongue.
We sign.

The stairs are dark and steep and narrow.
We trail our fingers down the dado,
descending for the beer and bingo,
our breathing fast and hot and shallow,
endorsed, accepted and elated,
CIU affiliated.

Our travels also took us east. It doesn't suit everyone.

Escape

There's a rabbit on the kitchen floor,
second one this week.
It does not wear blue trousers
and Mr McGregor doesn't live here any more.
Perhaps I'd better recognise it
if it had a head.

The cat's gone Rambo since we moved here,
following our bucolic dream,
outscreams the vixen, growls and paces,
got the bloodlust, bugger cream.

So, headless rabbit, what shall I do with you?
Make a hearty casserole?
Use your skin for baby bunting?
Save the daddy going hunting,
however much he might enjoy
the enterprise.

He likes the endless flat expanses,
witters on about the sky,
discusses birdsong, gets up early,
waves at tractors thundering by.

Please can we return to what we had
before the great uprooting?
I cannot stand it here.
I need a corner shop, congestion,
pavements, litter, Marks and Spencer's,
fully leaded air.

But I did meet others who found distance from the rest of the world a comfort.

Wish Fulfilled

She craves silence,
downy, enfolding,
like a winter duvet;
fifteen tog silence.

She longs for snow,
huge, untouched drifts,
away from interference,
busy ploughs and kindly shovels;
private snow,
for burrowing.

She desires deepest water,
oceans darker than the sharpness in her mouth,
depths where fish are blind,
and conversations rare;
yearns for peace.

Eventually the children leave
and she downsizes, moving east.

Searches flat, black, Norfolk fields,
the staggering white sky,
looks for signs of life, distinctly absent,
feels the old ties break.
No need for her conclusions to be spoken,
she hopes they will stay good and broken,
for a while;
sighs, settles, smiles.

Silence can wear many faces. They are often quite contented.

Teashop Mirror

They sit and sip,
gazing just beyond the vectors of eye contact,
no touch at knee or elbow, foot or hand,
in front of them two cakes, halved perfectly,
evidence of practised knifework.
Each will taste in silence, delighting in the other's choice.
Words would be redundant,
would add nothing to this gentle lifework
of sweet, shared experience.

I find that vignette of harmonious bliss instructive. Cake is a bringer of joy.

Cake

There is nothing better for an ache
than cake.
If the world is sad and dour,
reach for flour,
coconut and glacé cherry.
Make the most of them, make merry.
Cake is very, very, very
good for you.
You don't require a reason
to consume a raisin,
but one is very small
and may not give much ease at all,
so get a handful … and some nuts.
Have a ball.

But even cake cannot take away the irritations that beset those of us who have been around for a while and find some changes are a step too far.

Death of Soap

Can't carry on.
Hard to work out when it happened,
what the why, the how, the who,
but I can't listen to The Archers,
no matter what they say or do.

I guess that I was only in my twenties
when I became a dedicated listener.
Precarious job, precarious husband,
Worcestershire a world away,
but Ambridge was familiar territory.

Those fifteen minutes every evening,
whilst I made cheap, nutritious meals,
served to remind me, though it often seemed that way,
that the world had not gone mad,
just the bit where I was standing.

Life changed. The Archers were immutable.
I ironed to the Omnibus on Sundays,
first husband left behind, the second dead,
my home a semi with a view to sea,
and Ambridge in my head.

I was not the only one.
When duty called my boss away,
I would include synopses of our Midland fix
with minutes of the meetings
that kept our business running smooth.

I brought the Country Folk here to the Island,
listening at night when sleep just wouldn't come,
for fifty years, a close companion;
but recently there's been a change.
We are estranged.

So many dramas overlapping,
so busy, wild and unrestrained,
with every single human ill examined
for weeks on end, until I'm drained
of sympathy. When did the aliens land?

Or is it me? Have I become irascible,
Facebook denier, dinosaur,
resenting their continual, whining solipsism,
am I the bore?
It makes no difference.
I just don't like them any more.

So I will spend my time learning about real concerns. I read recently that there has been a study of the movement of discarded wellington boots in the North Sea. It has not yet been proposed that they should be reunited with their owners, who should have taken them home in the first place.

Destination

Consider the flow of the waves of the ocean,
the force of the wind and the tide,
as they gather our castoffs, our flotsam, our jetsam,
and send them to wander,
to wander like plankton,
useless detritus washed far and washed wide.

You would think that they'd gather according to origin,
with size, weight, and density key,
destined to join those great islands of shame
that we've seen in the papers,
that we've seen on TV,
that we know will destroy us, but it's not cut and dried.

The North Sea, it seems, is a graveyard for wellies.
Researchers are tracking their spoor.
Right boots go west and end up in Scotland,
left boots go east, to the opposite shore.
It's because of the difference,
the difference in shaping
the boot to the foot, nothing more.

Small things affect the form of the future,
small things dictate where we drift, where we land,
small things can alter the tides and the currents,
and the lines that we draw in the sand.

The Isle of Wight is making a stand with a bold conservation project. Sea eagles have been re-introduced to our shores.

Incident on the Isle of Wight

We left her
sitting on the cliff top,
reading the paper,
safe,
comfortable,

diminutive.

We had gone back to the car
to find binoculars
and the I Spy Book of Raptors.

When we returned,
our friend had disappeared.
We searched everywhere,
called the coastguard.

Giant talons round her shoulders,
padded by her woolly coat,
off to see the land of eagles,
above the clouds, beyond remote.

Hope she's back before the coach leaves.
Hope she doesn't miss the boat.

And while I'm on birdlife, there are crows up at Ventnor golf course with evil on their minds. They steal the golf balls. They steal sandwiches from zipped bags. The young are being taught to follow suit.

Mark Twain's Rules

There's a crow,
perched on a branch, out of range.
There's a crow,
old black corvid, nothing strange,
just a crow.

My tee shot's full and high and long,
loft and line like a poem, like a song,
like a day in the sun when you feel you belong.

So we walk,
down on the fairway, two hundred yards,
yes we walk,
and I know that the next bit won't be hard.
It will be where it should be,
exactly where it should be;
so we walk.

We look in the rough, in the sand, (there's no lake),
can't believe that a shot like that didn't take
me to well-nigh perfection …

There's a crow,
grinning like a bird-sized piece of trash.
There's a crow,
and he's added to his golf-themed bad-bird stash.
There's a crow,
and he swoops like a super-charged lightning flash
on unattended balls both orange and white.
There's a crow,
he'll get them on the ground or in mid flight.
There's a crow.

Footnote: Mark Twain remarked in passing, that picking up balls believed to be lost while they are still rolling is not sporting.

And finally, one for my mother, who died in May 2019. A couple of months beforehand she had issued very specific instructions about her passing, rejecting her previous plan to have exactly the same arrangements as our father.

And Also

For so many years a reflection of you,
doing the things that you liked to do,
agreeing, condoning, contriving;
that's wiving as we understood it,
we two.

But I've been without you for so many years,
making my own way in life.
Though I value the time that I stood by your side,
I feel now I'm more than just "wife".

I'm not an "and also". I've made up my mind
that my send-off will be full of fun, of the kind
you might well despise.

My children will sing and tell jokes.
There'll be flowery frocks and the blokes
won't be wearing black ties.

There'll be cake, there'll be sherry,
my friends will make merry,
no attempt to disguise

that it's all about me.

And when what is left has to rest in our plot,
I will go, I agreed.
But don't put "and also"
on our shiny black stone,
for I'm not an adjunct.

I stand alone.

I can find nothing in this book that mentions hip hop.
Bikes, yes, caution, yes, hip hop, no. Darn it! I'll have to
write another one …